JAMES CHALMERS

HEROES OF THE CROSS

JAMES CHALMERS

MARSHALLS

Marshall Morgan & Scott
1 Bath Street, London EC1V 9LB

Copyright © Marshall Morgan & Scott 1982

First published by Oliphants Ltd 1953
First issued in paperback in Lakeland 1963

This edition in Marshalls 1982
Impression number 10 9 8 7 6 5 4 3 2 1

ISBN: 0 551 00952 7

Printed in Great Britain by Richard Clay (The Chaucer Press) Ltd,
Bungay, Suffolk

CONTENTS

THE YOUNG TERROR

WHEN they brought young James Chalmers home rather more than half-drowned for the third time, his parents really began to wonder if it was possible to worry too much about the boy. If they were to go on like this, they would be old before their time through sheer, fruitless anxiety about a tragedy which might never happen—and which in fact never did happen.

In the end they came to accept his misadventures almost philosophically. But that seven-year-old boy really was a terror. They couldn't keep him out of the water. They whipped him: they walloped him—mother, father, the neighbours, and the fishermen down on the beach. But it was no good. The sea seemed to fascinate him, and since there was nothing—not even his father's braw right arm—of which he was afraid, naturally he was continually in trouble.

This, the third time, he was duly revived, stripped of his soaking clothes, and wrapped in warm blankets. I wonder his mother had the heart to assent to the walloping which was to come, as she looked at him. His thin, freckled face was a little pale, his black hair a wet, curly tangle; his brilliant dark eyes surveyed her over the mug

of hot tea. He looked such a tiny, frail scrap . . .
she wished he had a bit more flesh on him. . . .
But as a good parent should, she assented to
discipline.

The boy took his punishment philosophically:
after all, the sting was soon past, and no member
of the Argyll clan, however small, ought to greet
for a bit of a hurt . . . and it had been a glorious
adventure.

She sat and watched him, to all outward
appearances a stern, almost hard woman; but she
had a very tender heart, and dearly loved her
naughty, adventurous little boy. If the truth were
told, James probably inherited a good deal of his
high spirits from her, rather than from his quiet,
reserved father, for she was active and energetic,
and what is known as a strong character.

His father had just happened to be home at
Ardrishaig at the time. He was a stonemason,
and his work was at Inverary, twenty-three miles
away, so he was away all the week and usually
came home whenever he could to see his family,
little James and two daughters. So really James's
mother had more to do with his upbringing than
his father had. She made a good job of it, and he
loved her as well as having a wholesome respect
for her.

He knew her well enough, for instance, to take
with a pinch of salt her stern instruction to the
schoolmaster, when she had first taken him to
begin lessons: "Dinna spare the rod!"

As it happened, he managed to evade the rod

at school. But one day he earned for himself a far worse punishment.

James had an incurable "sweet tooth," and in the playground one day he stood and stared wistfully, meaningfully, at a big boy who was the happy possessor of a large bag of goodies.

"Like some?" the big boy asked.

James's answer need not be recorded.

"Right!" the big boy exclaimed—only because they were Scottish boys he said, "Reet." But we shall stick to English pronunciation as a rule, and try to remember that all James said all his life through, and all that his schoolfellows and friends in this part of his story said, was spoken with a Scottish lilt and pronunciation.

"Right! You chew this first, and you shall have fair halvers!" *This*, which James's senior proffered, was a lump of tobacco, very strong tobacco.

James didn't mind. He chewed with a will. After all, he was used to taking unpleasant things after many of his pleasures, so why not reverse the order for once? So he chewed on.

But, oh dear, by the time playtime was over James felt so ill. Grey-faced, sweating slightly, he staggered after his friends into the schoolroom. He just managed to reach his seat, and how thankfully he sat down. But the respite was not for long. Soon James's class was called up for a lesson, and his turn came to go up to the master's desk. He stood up unsteadily, took a step or two, staggered, and collapsed in an undignified bundle on the schoolroom floor.

The master picked him up in great concern, but one sniff made him understand. Tobacco, and at such a tender age! It was scandalous.

But plainly the laddie was in no state for more physical punishment. So instead of using the tawse the ingenious master sat him on his own desk, and completely eclipsed his shamed face with his own tall, chimney-pot hat, which was so big that the brim rested on the little boy's shoulders.

As a grown man James still remembered being "very ill," and we must hope the master's good hat did not suffer. Anyway James spent the rest of that day in his bed, feeling very sorry for himself, and having not the slightest hankering after the sweets which he had earned so dearly.

Still, he loved that schoolmaster; they all did in Ardrishaig, and everyone was sad when he left the village and the country, to go to Australia.

Everyone knew him, for he filled a special place in the village. They had no minister, and the only time they had a service was when someone came to baptise the children. But the schoolmaster used to hold a Sunday meeting whenever he could, and it was a great comfort to many of the people. Life is hard in a fishing village, and the nearest church was at Lochgilphead, miles away.

The people needed a good deal of teaching. They were terribly superstitious. Young James used to feel a chill down his spine every time a dog howled, because the folk down in the village said that "a crying dog was a sign of death."

They were so ignorant too. No one in the place

saw the funny side of the "cure" for whooping cough, even although the cure involved the use of a sorely puzzled donkey! The donkey was made to stand between the child's mother and another woman, and the poor terrified, whooping infant would be passed over the donkey's back, from hand to hand, and then—far worse—under his tummy!

But worse than ignorance was the drinking. When the fishermen came in with a catch they had a dram or two to celebrate: when the catch was sold they had another dram or two: and by the time they had all taken several drams in honour of the occasion they were fighting fit, and they fought. Then there would be arrests, and sore trouble and sorrow for wives and families.

Unhappily the next schoolmaster shared the village failing. He distinguished himself in James's memory by his lavish distribution of sweeties: but he was also famous—or infamous—for the frequent holidays and half-holidays which fell to the lot of the scholars owing to his great and lamentable liking for whisky.

Still, James's home was the sort of place where a bad influence could be offset. His mother was splendid, and his father's visits were always a joy; and it was a help in moments of temptation to think of the report which mother must make to him next time!

James was not yet eight when he had his next notable encounter with the waters of the loch.

By now he was not content with falling into the water: he must be upon it. If there was a boat to be had, that was fine. But if not, a log or a plank of wood had to serve, and the more dangerous it was the more exciting he found it.

Perhaps the happiest hours of his young life were spent with the hardy fishermen, who had a soft spot, one and all, for this bold little black-haired rascal; and sometimes they would take him out with them for short runs.

But that was not good enough. James and three of his friends decided they must build a boat for themselves. It was not as simple as it seemed: as soon as one difficulty was solved, another cropped up.

"Aw!" said James at last in disgust, "let's make ourselves one out of a herrin' box: there's plenty o' tar . . ."

So the herring box—and no doubt the four small boys as well—was liberally daubed with tar, and left to dry. It was soon ready and, of course, Master James Chalmers, the leader of the band, claimed first attempt at navigation.

Somewhere, somehow, they found a rope and tied it to one end of the box. In got James, and paddled himself out to deeper water. Then the three on shore pulled with a will, running parallel with the shore, and James had a few minutes of wildly exhilarating "cross-surf-riding" in that fishy, tarry box.

But it did not last long. Suddenly the three boys ashore went sprawling. The line had snapped, and

James's craft was adrift. The tide was strong, and the young sailor was carried out to sea by dangerous currents.

It was a good thing it was James in the boat. He kept his head whilst his three friends ran for help, and thanks to a brave boatman he was safely rescued. But what followed upon that adventure, by way of parental reprisal, is a tale that has never been told. Whatever it was, he earned it!

Another excitement, of a very different kind, was a visit to his father at Inverary. It was wonderful to stay in his father's lodgings, and be made a fuss of by the landlady. More exciting still, to go down to the new quay that was being built and see how the great stones, which his father had hewn, were fitting in to the pattern.

Oddly enough for such a little boy, what James remembered best of all at Inverary was the church. There wasn't a church at home, of course, and although this was only a small place, young James was enormously impressed. It probably gave his simple faith a greater reality to see that little building crowded to the doors with people who believed the very same truths that he had been taught at home.

But it wasn't long before the whole family settled down to a more usual sort of life. They moved to Glenary, which was near enough to Inverary for James's father to go to his work each day.

The Chalmers children used to go to school

three miles down the glen: and hard going it was in the bitter winter months, when the river Aray was a rushing, tumbling torrent, but a delight in the spring and summer.

From points all along the road between the town of Glenary and the school, more and more children would come to swell the band. Presumably the little girls made their way sedately together. The boys *made their way together,* but not sedately. The Mintos, the Blakes and others from the town made one gang: James and other boys from the glen made the second, and many a fight they had. They usually began with divots of turf: but all too soon tempers rose, then stones began to fly. Black eyes and bruises were only too common; and as the schoolmaster, Mr. McArthur, had an eagle eye, stripes invisible were soon added to the bruises visible.

On the whole the Glenary schoolmaster was a just man. Only once in James's memory was he otherwise. James was accused of a crime which he had not committed. He flatly denied it; but Mr. McArthur was convinced he was guilty, and soon his temper was roused by the apparently bare-faced lies of a usually honest boy. Poor James had several canes broken over him that day, and he went home with a sore heart and a sore back. But he wasn't going to confess to something he hadn't done, not if old McArthur broke fifty canes over him!

When at last the truth came out years later, James was a grown man in the South Pacific, and it was not till thirty years after that a very aged Mr. McArthur with a quavering voice made his apologies to the famous missionary he had once unjustly caned.

II

GROWING PAINS

JAMES soon regained his good name at school. He was only ten at the time, but he showed the courage and sense of a grown man.

The boys were on their way home from school in brilliant sunshine, after a morning of torrential rain. The Aray was in full spate after the downpour, and all the little streamlets were tumbling and raging down, to add to the volume of water.

The schoolboys chatted excitedly, exhilarated by the sunshine and the madly tumbling waters. Then suddenly there was a shout: "Johnnie Minto's in the watter!"

James and the others rushed to the side of the bridge aghast—but James took off his jacket as he ran. In a trice he was down under the bridge, holding on by the timbers on the under side.

He was just in time. Rolling over and over in the muddied water, terrified, helpless, came young Johnnie. But hanging on firmly with one hand, James stretched out the other and grabbed him by his clothes. The pull of the water, with the weight of the helpless boy as well, was terrible: but somehow he managed to ease himself and his burden into the flood, so that they were both carried down river to where James saw a branch overhanging the water.

Frantically he grasped it, and in a very short time he and Johnnie were helped up the bank, breathless, soaked, gasping, but blessedly safe.

That time when James Chalmers came home soaked to the skin, there was no walloping! And he was not too shy to relish the public announcement of his achievement next day at school, or the hearty cheers which followed the headmaster's telling of the story.

Little wonder that by the time he was fourteen James was appointed the leader of the local Robin Hood band—whose exploits are best left to the imagination.

James wasn't a bad lad. He was brimful of high spirits and mischief, but he had the people at home to think of. He couldn't grieve his parents: they were so good and so understanding. For instance, although they belonged to the Established Church of Scotland—and in those days if you belonged to a church in Scotland you *belonged*—when James asked their permission to join the Sunday school of the United Presbyterian Church, because "some of the laddies at school go there," they didn't mind a bit.

As a matter of fact, James's father thought the world of Mr. Meikle, the United Presbyterian minister: and he was a good shepherd of young souls. On one of the few occasions when James didn't turn up on Sunday afternoon, he took the trouble to walk over three miles up the hill to the Chalmers home to make sure the boy wasn't ill.

Something very important happened in that Sunday school one day. The older boys had had their lesson in the vestry, an honour to which their dignity entitled them: then they had marched back to the chapel for singing, and for a talk to the whole school.

Mr. Meikle took from his breast pocket a copy of the *United Presbyterian Record*.

"I'm going to read to you all today a most interesting letter from a missionary in Fiji!" he announced.

Some of the children just heard one more missionary report and forgot it. But James listened with both ears and with all his heart, for this story of adventuring for Christ thrilled him to the very soul.

"I wonder," said Mr. Meikle slowly, when he had finished, "if there is a boy here this afternoon who will become a missionary, and by and by bring the Gospel to the cannibals . . ."

James Chalmers spoke to nobody after Sunday school that afternoon. His cronies stared at him as he marched straight out of the building and away down the road without a word.

"Weel, an' what's the matter wi' him?" they asked one another in perplexity.

James had a lot to think about as he strode on. When he had heard that challenge he had said

in his heart, "Yes, God helping me! *And I will!*"
The more he thought the more vital it all became
to him: so that when he came to the bridge above
the mill he shinned over the wall, and kneeling
down, there and then he prayed that God would
accept him and make him a missionary to the
heathen.

As a matter of fact God did nothing of the sort.
God doesn't make people into things: *He helps
them to become things.* But for a while, after the
first thrill had worn off, James wasn't in the mood
to be helped, and, sad to say, in a short time he
had forgotten all about the whole matter.

School days passed, and he began to earn his
own living as a clerk in a solicitor's office; and
unhappily, like so many of us, he seemed to
think he was getting a bit big for Sunday school
and church. Sometimes he went: sometimes he
stayed away. Then he went less often, and stayed
away more.

He certainly wasn't particularly happy: he
couldn't bear to meet good Mr. Meikle and hear
him repeat what his own conscience was telling
him. In fact, more than once when he saw the
short-sighted minister coming his way, he clam-
bered over the wall until the coast was clear.

This definitely was not one of the best times of
James's life. He was the ringleader in half the
mischief in the town, so that if there was any
trouble he got the blame, whether he was guilty
of it or not. You know how it is: "Give a dog a
bad name, and hang him!"

He was facing a real problem in his spiritual
life, to make matters worse. He had had so much
of the Catechism at home and at school, so much
questioning about the Bible, that it was something of an overdose: in those days in the
Highlands there was a lot of teaching about the
terrible judgments of God, and very little about
His love.

Mr. Meikle, it is true, didn't preach like that:
he knew that his God was loving, as well as holy
and just, and he wouldn't teach anything else.

But other people didn't think as Mr. Meikle
did; it worried and perplexed James so much
that for a time he gave up his religious life
altogether; and it was at that time that he came
perilously near to breaking his mother's heart.

When he was sixteen he grew weary of office
life in a little Highland town. He must have
adventure: he must see life, and the upshot was
that he planned with two friends of his to run
away to sea.

Everything was arranged. The meeting place
was fixed, and after an evening of unbearable
excitement and anticipation James went early to
bed, got his bundle of clothes ready, and settled
down to wait for the early morning. With the first
light he was going to slip away down to the coast
where a certain little boat was ready.

But he couldn't do it. He didn't have a wink of
sleep all that night: he could only think of what
this thing would do to his mother. Thank God,
he wasn't callous; if he hadn't been the loving,

tender-hearted boy he was, in manhood he could
never have gained the love of fierce, unruly
savages.

So the next morning there were only two
bitterly sad families in Inverary: James Chalmers
stayed at home.

He was eighteen before he was ready for God
to help him. He wouldn't go to church: he
wouldn't go to Sunday school: and he had even
gone so far as to make plans with some of his
friends to interfere with a series of special meetings
which Mr. Meikle had organised. They had
made up their minds that no one was going to be
converted in *their* town.

But someone was. One of the first of the meetings
was to be held at seven o'clock in the loft over the
carpenter's workshop, and early that evening
Chalmers happened to call at an older friend's
house.

"Ye ought to be going to the meeting the
neet!" said his friend. "The evangelists are fine
fellows: from the North of Ireland they are . . ."

James pished and pshawed, but it was no use.
He couldn't get out of it without being openly
rude to an older man. His friend clinched the
matter by thrusting upon him a small Bible to use
at the service, and somehow he found himself
meekly setting off in the pouring rain for the
carpenter's shop.

When he got to the bottom of the stairs to the
loft the people had started singing a hymn, and
the way they sang it—"All people that on earth

do dwell," it was—made James Chalmers resist his natural longing to put miles between himself and the place, and up those stairs he went.

When the meeting was over he hurried down again, back to his friend's house, and gave him his Bible without a word. What he heard had given him so much to think about that he simply could not speak.

When *some* people give their hearts to the Lord Jesus Christ it is like a child coming home to its mother. With others it is harder: it was with James. For a few days he was altogether miserable; he knew he couldn't go on as he was, but he didn't want to give in to these new longings.

But he did it in the end: he had to. He knew that he was sinful, and he was desperately afraid of being lost to God. So in the end he took his troubles to good Mr. Meikle, and Mr. Meikle sent him to the Bible, where it is promised that "the blood of Jesus Christ . . . cleanseth us from all sin." The end of it all was that James Chalmers became a true Christian.

He was radiant: everyone must know about his Saviour. He preached at meetings, he preached in cottages, he taught in the Sunday school he had left. In fact he became such an ardent witness for the Lord Jesus Christ that he forgot mere common sense; he quite wore himself out and was soon seriously unwell.

But he quickly learned the right use of the body he had dedicated to the Lord, and it was not long before there came back into his mind the memory of his promise to God, that *he* would be the boy who would become a missionary to the cannibals.

It wasn't an easy thing for James. His parents were poor, and couldn't afford a university course for him. How could he prepare for the mission field? Mr. Meikle promised to help him with his Latin, mathematics and other subjects, which was something; but what was more to the point, he told him how many Christian students kept themselves and paid for their college fees— by working as missionaries of the Glasgow City Mission and studying between whiles.

Soon James was in Glasgow, and many valuable lessons he learned there. Years later, after he had been living for some time among the fiercest cannibals, he confessed that the people of Glasgow had been far harder to deal with— tougher and more vicious—so in a way those months were good training, good discipline.

Now James met in Glasgow a man from the South Sea Islands, Dr. George Turner, who was seeing to the publication of an edition of the Samoan Scriptures.

"Don't wait!" Dr. Turner advised. "Apply to the London Missionary Society, and see if *they* won't send you out. They put their candidates through college and missionary training . . ."

So James applied to the London Missionary Society, with some trepidation, and he was accepted; after only eight months in Glasgow, a few weeks after his twenty-first birthday, he made his way south to learn to be a missionary among what he and his kind call "the Sassenachs!"

III

"THAT SCOTSMAN"

BECAUSE the men at Cheshunt College were to become missionaries, it did not mean that they had no sense of fun. Of course some of them were genuine sobersides, but on the whole these servants of God had high spirits as well as a high purpose.

Some were true scholars, men who loved study for its own sake and who were never happier than when they were lost in their books. Others —James Chalmers to the fore among them— worked faithfully at the subjects they must cover to fit them for the mission field, but it was working to pass examinations, and not scholarship for its own sake.

The result was, of course, that James and his like found that they had time on their hands. For instance, there was the interval between college tea and supper, when the scholars retired to their studies. James Chalmers and his friends roamed about the college in search of mischief—which they rarely failed to find, greatly to the disturbance of the serious-minded fraternity.

One evening at last Chalmers provoked his

victims to retaliation. There was a measure of con-
fabulation in the scholarly studies, and the next
evening there was drastic action against the
ringleader of the mischief-makers.

Tea was over, and there was the usual quiet in
Chalmers's corridor for a little while, and in one
particular study half a dozen of his customary
victims waited in complete silence.

"*Here he comes!*" someone whispered, and they
heard the stealthy footsteps of the Scot, bent
upon trouble.

He got it. There was silence as they watched
the door handle turn, the door open: and then
they pounced.

All Chalmers's wiry strength and Scottish
determination could not help him in the hands of
this group of resolute men, who made him
captive and bundled him back into his own study.
Fighting furiously, shouting and laughing, he
was thrust inside, and the door was shut upon him.

Chalmers was surprised at the mildness of this
retaliation, and perhaps a little annoyed at the
indignity of being "shut in his room." But wonder
soon gave place to discomfort, acute discomfort.

Outside the closed door, held firmly shut, the
avengers were busy. One of them disappeared to
fulfil the special part allotted to him—of which
more hereafter—and the others, not without
difficulty, began to poke into the keyhole some
reddish-brown, granular substance.

"Got the matches?" someone whispered, and
the matches were produced, and—again not

without difficulty—the substance was set alight. It smouldered only, but with the aid of a little puffing, its generous, smoky emanations were soon passing freely into Chalmers's room.

Now cayenne pepper, for that is what it was, burns at first with a pleasantly aromatic odour. It takes a few seconds for the hot, peppery fumes to become active. But when they do . . .

The men outside the door were soon hugging themselves with delighted anticipations as they heard Chalmers coughing a little.

Soon he was spluttering and gasping, and they heard him make a rush for the door. But there were too many holding on outside, and the fumes were too thick.

Next they heard him rush for the window, still coughing and choking. They heard the clatter and scrape of a hastily thrown up sash, and they all grinned broadly in anticipation.

Then came the climax of their plot. The missing man had gone into action. From his station on the roof exactly above Chalmers's window he could hardly fail in his aim, and he didn't. Fair and square on Chalmers's head, as he was drawing in great gulps of the sweet evening air, there descended a douche—a most liberal douche—of clear, cold water, from a brimming bucket.

No doubt it quenched some of his sufferings from the peppery fumes, but it did not at all quench his thirst for practical joking. The opinion of the scholarly band was that he had benefited not at all by the lesson.

There was, for instance, the apparition of the great brown bear. Chalmers had a missionary friend in London who numbered among his curios an enormous bear's skin, complete with head and claws. This friend was a curate, so we will assume that when Chalmers pleaded with him for permission to borrow the skin he did not ask the reason why.

With the help of one or two of Chalmers's confederates, it was smuggled by night into the college, and the next evening the stage was set.

It was at the close of a quiet evening: prayers were over and the men were having their supper in the dining hall. Suddenly the door was flung wide, and in shambled a huge bear, roaring tremendously. On hind legs, with a peculiar rolling gait, it made its way among the startled students.

It was a fastidious bear: it noticeably avoided the more robust, vigorous type of man, and took to its embraces a quiet, studious fellow, who probably thought his last hour had come.

But he survived, and just after the lights went out, he found himself released with no bones broken. In the darkness there was a glorious scrimmage, with the shambling monster chasing one man after another. It was some time before someone found a box of matches and lit the gas again . . . and it was much later still before a suitably punished Chalmers was released from his disguise.

Not all the rules of Cheshunt College or of the

New River Company could keep James away from the water which ran through the lovely grounds. There was no boat, so he made himself a raft: and it was one of the college sights to see "that crazy Scotsman, Chalmers," manœuvring his craft, running from end to end with his pole, punting it along, occasionally running right over the end and disappearing into the water! That "raftsmanship" was no part of his curriculum, but it was to be of good service to him in his missionary life.

For all his pranks and practical jokes, his noisy high spirits, the students liked James Chalmers. His freckled face was full of open kindliness: one of the men once said, "If you're a wet blanket and you stay in his company long, you become dry!"

With his sense of fun there went a sense of the presence of God: when his rich voice was heard at the students prayer meeting, pleading with the Lord in broad Scots, many a man marvelled at his fervour, and longed to know the depth of spiritual life he knew.

More than that, Chalmers was not only eloquent in prayer, he was good tempered in everyday life: and sometimes the two things do not go together.

It was not that his life was easy. Study was hard work for James; and in addition to their studies the students were each given charge of a little village church. Possibly it was because he was tall, strong, and lithe, but he was given the

one farthest away from the college. It was eight
miles off, and those eight miles had to be walked:
the railway was no help at all.

But if there had been convenient trains,
Chalmers couldn't afford to ride. For here was his
greatest trial: he was always hard up. Most of the
students had at least a little money of their own:
but he was quite dependent upon what the
London Missionary Society allowed him: and
because the authorities did not quite understand
the situation, the allowance they made him
barely paid for his washing, lighting, and fuel.

It was better after the first year, because
second-year students had preaching engage-
ments, and their fees were pooled and shared out.
In student language, second year men were "on
the box," and Chalmers had his share.

But the first twelve months were bitterly hard.
James had his full share of honest Scots indepen-
dence, and it was miserable to be literally penni-
less among a crowd of men who all had at least a
little money in their pockets.

But he battled bravely on, managing somehow;
and he even had the pluck to admit that the hardship—and it *was* hardship—was splendid training
for a missionary.

That easier second year came and went, and
Chalmers finished his course, though not his
missionary training. Farquhar House, Highgate,
was specially established by the London Missionary Society as a place where students might
round off their preparation for the field.

There were twenty-seven of these earnest but extremely vigorous young men in Chalmers' first year, and the principal, Dr. John Wardlaw, and his wife needed all their considerable stock of patience in dealing with them—particularly after the advent of James Chalmers.

It was only a few days after his first term had begun that Mrs. Wardlaw came running into the students' common room, seriously alarmed, for the whole house seemed to be shaking. But it was only Mr. Chalmers entertaining the rest by a performance of a highland fling!

Mrs. Wardlaw is hardly to be blamed for the true story which went round the college a few days later. Very early the next Sunday morning everyone in the place was awakened by a loud, shattering noise. Every window in the building rattled: doors were flung open, and loud anxious queries as to *"Whatever's that?"* passed from room to room.

Then there was a moment of silence, and Mrs. Wardlaw's voice came plaintively from the stairs:

"I suppose it is Mr. Chalmers at one of his noisy games again!"—and she was perfectly serious.

We can well imagine the irreverent guffaws over the breakfast table next morning, when it was learned that the commotion was caused by a terrible explosion *in the gunpowder mills fifteen miles away*.

If there was less time for practical joking at Highgate—and there was—the work was much

more to Chalmers's liking. It was good to be
preparing for practical work on the mission field:
to be doing a short medical course, so that he
might win the people's confidence by improving
their health: to be gaining a certain amount of
mechanical knowledge that he might be able to
help himself in uncivilised parts of the world:
to be thrilled by the history of missionary work,
past and present, in all parts of the globe, and
challenged by the study of the heathen religions—
religions which he, James Chalmers, might be
sent to combat.

When the year at Highgate was over,
Chalmers and his friend Saville had to pass
some months of waiting while their ship was
making ready. They spent the months very happily in the home of the Rev. George Gill, a
former missionary to Raratonga—the South Sea
island to which Chalmers had been appointed by
the London Missionary Society. Saville was going
to another island, Huahaine, so together they
studied languages diligently, and waited with
eager anticipation.

At last the *John Williams* was ready, and
Chalmers and Saville were given their orders.
They must make themselves ready for the solemn
service of ordination, and for marriage—for both
men were engaged by now—that they might have
staunch comradeship on the field.

While young James Chalmers had been falling
in and out of the water at Ardrishaig, happy and
altogether irresponsible, a little five-year-old

motherless girl had had to learn to be "little mother" to three smaller children.

While James Chalmers had been playing schoolboy pranks in Inverary, that same little girl, now fourteen, had left her brothers and sisters to look after a widowed grandmother.

She was Jane Hercus, a splendid little Christian servant of others: and she grew up to be a splendid Christian woman—a bit solemn at times perhaps, but who can wonder at that, after the sorrows and burdens of her childhood? Still, she was staunch, and for all her quiet, almost timid manner, as brave as a lion.

Certainly she had enough sense of fun for James Chalmers to fall in love with her when he met her in Glasgow, before he went to Cheshunt: it was not *only* her goodness and her earnest faith which appealed to him.

Not long after his twenty-fourth birthday James Chalmers married Jane Hercus: two days later he was ordained, and the Rev. James and Mrs. Chalmers were ready to sail away for the South Seas, a fine pair of fully equipped missionaries, happily married, and longing for only one thing, that the *John Williams*—a clipper ship still building in Aberdeen—might be speedily completed.

In January 1866 she sailed, and surely the happiest among her passengers were two newly-married couples, the Chalmers and the Savilles.

IV

SEA PERILS

"Ye're the best sailor of all the leddies, Jeanie!
And better than a gude many of the menfolk
too!" James Chalmers spoke proudly to his wife
as they stood together on deck, enjoying the
sweet air and the sunshine.

The lovely weather was welcome. The begin-
nings of the voyage in the cold of early January
had been frightful. Before they were out of the
Channel they had met a furious gale—so furious
that twenty-one other ships had been sunk.
The *John Williams* had survived, but she was so
badly damaged that they had to put back into
Weymouth for repairs, and most of the passengers
had been very much the worse for wear.

All the others had stayed in Weymouth while
the repairs were being carried out, but James
and Jeanie had preferred to remain on board,
and they had a quiet happy time together in
spite of the bad weather.

Once they had sailed again they soon reached
sunnier regions, and the rest of the voyage to
Australia was delightful.

James was in his element: he was what they call
"a man's man," and soon he was perfectly at
home with the sailors, lending a hand on deck

where he could, paying solemn attention to their
sea yarns, and carefully concealing the twinkle
in his eye over those which were more than
usually outrageous.

He gained their confidence and their admi-
ration. There were no protests when he suggested
a Bible class for them. That Bible class bore fruit
in the conversion of some of the toughest among
the crew, and soon there was a fo'c'sle prayer
meeting as well.

It was May before they reached Australia, and
they had a wonderful welcome from Christian
friends there. Best of all, Jeanie's father, who had
moved with his family to New Zealand before
her marriage, came to Adelaide to meet them,
and carried Jeanie off back home with him for
three happy weeks.

While she was gone James visited Christian
friends in various places, among them some
retired missionaries from Raratonga: we can
imagine how eagerly he questioned them about
the place, the work and the people.

It was well that they had those quiet, happy
weeks before setting sail for Raratonga, for the
devil had obviously made up his mind that James
and Jeanie Chalmers needed watching: if they
arrived at their destination they were going to
upset a good many of his plans.

From the time they set sail from Australia
everything seemed to be against them. They were
to call on their way at the island of Niue with
supplies for the missionaries there, Mr. and Mrs.

Lawes. But before long the *John Williams* struck a hidden reef outside Aneiteum. The captain did not think that there was much damage to his ship, but it meant a long wait before the tide shifted her, so most of the missionaries went ashore.

James and Jeanie and the Savilles stayed on board, and while the ladies kept the captain's wife company, the men worked as hard as any of the sailors: and it *was* hard work. Day and night the pumps must be kept going, while the missionaries helped the sailors to lighten the ship by discharging the cargo. It was three days before they were ready for the final stage of the operation.

A goodly company of natives was mustered well to one side of the deck, and they stood to attention and waited for the missionary's word: "Go!"

With a mighty shout Chalmers and Saville and the rest ran to the far side, leaped up in the air and down again. It worked. Gently the *John Williams* slid off the reef and into the deep water.

But the pumps had to be kept going all the way back to Sydney—for she had to return for repairs before they could safely make for Niue again.

When at last they did reach that island, they could not come near to the shore, for here, too, was a dangerous coral reef: so the captain kept her well away, and the supplies of Mr. and Mrs. Lawes were unloaded into the boats. The generous natives of Niue did not send the boats back empty: on the return journey they were laden with presents of yams, taro, bananas and cocoanuts, which were stowed away below with much appreciation.

That night it was calm and quiet. There was a heavy swell on, but the *John Williams* was well out to sea so they all felt perfectly happy and restful, captain, passengers and crew.

The crew were particularly joyous: their pet Nellie, a Newfoundland dog, had presented them with a dozen little furry puppy bundles, and as the present situation made small demands upon their seamanship, they had plenty of time for admiring her and her offspring.

But there came an interruption. Captain Williams was not exactly anxious, but there *was* a heavy swell, and the ship did seem to be drifting landward a little.

"Lower away the whaleboat!" his order suddenly rang out in the dusk.

So the whaleboat was sent ahead, well manned: tow ropes were fixed, and Captain Williams watched to see the drift of his ship checked. But still she went astern.

"Lower away the pinnace!" he commanded: and the pinnace and the whaleboat pulled together. Still there was no result. The *John Williams* was very slowly but very steadily going nearer to the shore, nearer to the cruel rocks of the reef.

"Lower the gig!" The new order was edged with real anxiety, and was obeyed with utmost promptitude. But even the three boats filled with valiant men exerting their full strength, could not arrest that fatal drift.

By now everyone on board was acutely anxious. Rockets were fired to warn those ashore that the schooner was in danger; they waited, tense and fearful. In the darkness the white surf could be plainly seen breaking over the reef; and Captain Williams knew that the time had come for him to look to the safety of the seventy lives entrusted to his care.

He prayed first with the missionaries: they all prayed with all their hearts. The *John Williams* was a missionary ship: could it be that God would let her sink when she was dedicated to His service? Oh, how they prayed. Although we cannot always understand why, even God's "no" answers are good answers: and in this case it *was* a "no" answer.

The gig was called alongside now, and the ladies were handed in. Next came the whaleboat and the pinnace; soon the men missionaries and the crew—and Nellie, with eight of her offspring in a bucket and the rest inside one of the sailors' shirts—were taken off the ship.

At the last moment Captain Williams almost refused to go.

"I can't leave her! I can't leave her!" he muttered, when nearly everyone else was in the boats. "*I cannot leave her!*"

"But, man, you must!" Chalmers's voice was low and desperately earnest. "This is nothing but heathen folly. Think of your wife: think of the good work you'll be able to do for the Master in the future. You must come!"

He was nearly heartbroken, but he came: and the fact that he lost nearly everything he possessed did not cause him half so much sorrow as the loss of his ship.

For lost she was. The three boats lay off at a safe distance only for a short time before they heard a terrible, grinding crash: they could see nothing in the darkness, but they could only too well imagine the good ship's plight as the waves crashed her again and again on the cruel rocks.

The women cried openly and unashamedly: because it was so very dark no one could see the men's faces, but probably there was not a dry eye among them.

They were in sad plight: they had no food, no water, and only a few of them had any change of clothing. Chalmers had on only trousers, a shirt, a pair of socks, and the watch which the poor folk of Glasgow had presented to him. To make matters worse there was a sudden downpour of tropical rain, and in a matter of seconds they were all drenched to the skin, and very, very cold.

But the devil had gone as far as the Creator of heaven and earth would allow him. We don't know why he was allowed to go so far: but we are quite content to believe that God knew exactly what He was about.

The people on shore had seen the rockets, and

it was not long before the miserably uncomfortable occupants of the soaking boats saw cheerful lights in the darkness, lit for their guidance, cheer and encouragement by those on shore.

They rowed painfully but steadily toward land, until they found themselves near the opening in the reef.

In spite of the risk, a canoe put off from the shore and made its way through the opening and toward the boats. Two or three at a time the people from the boats were helped into the rocking canoe, and were paddled through the opening in the reef. The canoe seemed such a *very* frail craft: the opening so *very* small in the torch-lit darkness: and white foam which hid the cruel rocks seemed so *very* close on either hand as they were paddled through.

But by half-past four in the morning all were safely landed: and not one of those seventy sad, weary, drenched people could begin to tell how grateful they were for the tender loving kindness of Mr. and Mrs. Lawes and their helpers. As for Nellie, she had very little to say: with twelve hungry young ones busy making up for lost time, she had no thought for anything but a sleepy, comfortable silence, after a hearty feed.

The end of the journey to Raratonga was somewhat romantic, even if it was safe. For want of a better ship Chalmers and Saville chartered a brig to take them to their stations, which was very far from being a mission ship. She was a notorious vessel, captained by a bully and a pirate,

Captain Bully Hayes. But even this bad man came under Chalmers's spell.

Before they had embarked he and the captain had become good friends. One afternoon just before they sailed Chalmers made a request:

"Captain Hayes, I hope you will have no objection to our having morning and evening services on board, and twice on Sabbaths. All the services will be short, and only those who would like to come need attend."

Instead of exploding in a volley of oaths—which might have been expected of him—the pirate gave willing consent.

"Certainly, certainly!" he said affably. "My ship is a missionary ship now, and I hope you'll feel it so": and he added grimly, "*All* on board will attend those services!"

"Only if they are inclined," Chalmers said thankfully, but firmly. He was not going to have any man driven to a service at the rope's end.

For all his bad reputation and his bullying ways, Bully Hayes was a good host to the missionaries. It was only when he lost his temper that the true man showed through; then he was like a madman, and those who had any sense at all kept out of his way.

He was under no illusions about himself, and at times he was ashamed. "If only you were near me," he once said to Chalmers, "I should certainly become a new man and lead a different life!"

But the sad truth is that Chalmers's nearness

had only ended a few days before Bully Hayes nearly killed one of the men on board—and the weapon he used was the bag of money with which the missionary had paid for the voyage!

V

RARATONGA

CONVERSATION is not easy when one is balanced in an uneasy sitting position on the shoulders of a native who is striding jauntily through not particularly shallow water to the shore. So when James Chalmers's supporter demanded of him, the day that he landed on Raratonga:

"What fellow name belong you?" the answer was not too clear.

Certainly the Raratongan did not hear it clearly: and in any case it was a hard name for a simple man to twist round his tongue.

So when, as was the custom, he roared out the name of the new missionary to announce him to those on the shore, the word "Chalmers" had become:

"Tamate! Tamate!" and "Tamate" James Chalmers became, from that day on, until his life in the South Seas came to an end. The best phonetic spelling we can manage is Ta-mah-tay.

It was in May, and he would soon be twenty-five. Perhaps it was as well that his journey to this lovely island had not been too peaceful, and that he had had his fill of adventure: for he was to stay on Raratonga for ten years of quiet mission station work, among a people who had been under the influence of the Gospel for two generations. He might have found the routine dull and disappointing after all his dreams of immediate contact with fierce cannibals in strange islands unknown to any other white man. But as it was, he and Jeanie were reasonably content to wait for their great adventure: and certainly the waiting meant that he came to understand the hearts of these wild people, as well as their language, as he might never have done otherwise.

In any case, no one could have quarrelled with such a lovely place as Raratonga.

Fully sixty miles before they reached the island they had been able to see the tops of its highest mountains, and as they drew nearer they gazed in wonder at its beauties.

It was as lovely a coral island as any story-teller could invent. Surrounding it was the great coral reef, nearly bare at low tide, but a glory of silvery spray when the mighty waves of the Pacific, more than twenty feet high, crashed one after another against it.

Inside the reef the water was quieter, and here and there were lovely lagoons and deep natural harbours, one of them with four tiny green islets of its own.

On the shore a white, sandy beach stretched to a rich belt of land covered with groves of chestnut, coconut, breadfruit and banana trees. Between that fertile belt and the hills lay the taro swamps, behind them rich slopes and rugged green valleys: more hills, then valleys again, ascending in a riot of natural loveliness to the wild mountains.

Not many years before this place had been a place of horrors: but the preaching of the Gospel had changed a fierce people, utterly given up to cruelty, vice and cannibalism, into a law-abiding and partly civilised race.

By now there were churches with native pastors at five settlements, and a fully-fledged mission station at Avarua. The missionaries in charge when Tamate and Jeanie arrived were a Mr. and Mrs. Krause, and they gave the new workers a royal welcome. It was high time they came: Mr. Krause had been ill for a long while, and it was urgently necessary that he should be relieved.

Chalmers had been appointed to a place on the other side of the island, Ngatangiia, but because of the uncertain attitude of the people at that particular time, it was decided that they should work from Avarua for the present.

This did not at all suit the Ngatangiia people: one morning a great crowd of them came marching up to the mission house, shouting and dancing, and demanding *their* missionary. Poor Mr. Krause was really not fit to stand the commotion: he did not know what to do at all, and he was almost in a panic.

There was only one thing for Chalmers to do: take matters into his own hands.

"Look, Mr. Krause," he exclaimed. "Let us go with them just to see their settlement. We'll just stay with them for a few days, and then come back . . ."

"But . . . but . . . but . . . " Mr. Krause could hardly speak for excited worry.

Chalmers swept the "buts" aside: after all, if they were going to work among the Raratongans they must show them that they trusted them. Jeanie was agreeable, so it was all arranged, and soon eight lusty blacks were literally running away with the missionaries!

Chairs had been lashed to poles, and no sooner were James and Jeanie seated, than off the bearers ran, bumping and jolting, out of Avarua.

Chalmers was allowed to walk once they were outside the village, and they both had the kindest welcome at Ngatangiia. Those few happy days were invaluable: they taught Tamate and his wife much about the people, and they taught the people to love Tamate and his wife.

Six weeks later the Krauses left for home, and Tamate was left in charge of the work on Raratonga. It was a full, busy life. There was the preaching at Avarua and the settlement churches. There was the work of the Institution, where native teachers were trained, and the chiefs of the settlements were educated that they might better govern their own peoples. There were

classes for the women for Jeanie to teach: there
were Bible classes for all types; there were in-
quirers' classes; there was the boys' school. There
were prayer meetings and services of all kinds:
there was translation work to be done, and a very
out-of-date printing press to be persuaded to do
its work. Then there was medical work, and the
training of the mothers, that the babies might be
properly reared.

There was a never-ceasing battle against drink,
by teaching, by example, by the formation of
very primitive temperance societies. Not only did
Jeanie have so much work to do that she and
her husband very rarely saw each other during
the day: such events as the advent of a drunken
chief who had to be scolded, and dosed with strong
tea and bicarbonate of soda, were part of her
general routine.

But Jeanie was gallant, capable, energetic—
a true missionary's wife, and five full, happy
years seemed to pass very swiftly.

Of course, the missionaries were not always
well: the climate was fruitful of fevers, and there
were days and weeks of sickness. But they kept
going somehow. Chalmers was physically tough,
and he found that his best cure when he had been
unwell was to take a trip up into the mountains
as soon as he could walk again. Very soon he
could boast that he had been on every mountain
top in Raratonga, and had explored most of the
lovely valleys.

As for Jeanie, when she wasn't well she battled

on until she felt better again, and Tamate never knew of the days when she was not in the "excellent health and spirits" with which he credited her in his letters home.

At the end of that first five years the London Missionary Society made an important decision. North of the mainland was New Guinea, such a large island as to be virtually a continent. Now it was decided to open the mission there.

It was an island absolutely unknown to the white peoples, inhabited by cannibals who did not even know of the existence of spiritual needs. It was a field after Tamate's and Jeanie's own hearts, *but the Mission directors in London said that Chalmers and his wife could not be spared from Raratonga.*

Yet neither of them rebelled. It was a disappointment of the first order, but they accepted it, and did all they could to help those who *were* going. Six teachers from the Institution were chosen to accompany the missionaries, and they and their wives were as well equipped by Tamate and *his* wife as loving concern and Christian zeal could devise. So they saw the pioneers off, and stayed behind to work on Raratonga.

Tamate was most deeply loved there now, and Jeanie too.

"Even the drunkards rather like the missionary!" Chalmers wrote, and well they might. He strove continually to help them, and to win them from their temptations.

He was so quick to seize opportunities. A few

of the younger men from the bush had been to Tahiti, and had seen military drill there. No sooner did they come home to Raratonga than they gathered their boon companions together to drill as well as to drink.

One day Chalmers came home to find a band of these wild, lawless heavy drinkers drilling outside the mission station.

"Oho!" he exclaimed—in Raratongan, of course. "A volunteer band. You meet for drill: now you must come to church as a company!"

The outcome was that some of them began to attend church parade. What was their pride when once or twice in his sermons Tamate referred to the Volunteer Band!

Soon more of them were there in the church on Sundays. Soon they had less money for drink because they wanted "respectable" clothing for church parade. Then they began to work on their land to get more money for still smarter clothes.

There grew up a Volunteer Bible class, a Volunteer English class . . . until these wild young bush men found themselves developing into regular church-goers. They weren't all converted in a twelvemonth: the devil doesn't let people go as quickly as that. But at least they were hearing all about the Lord Jesus Christ, and there was not a man among them who did not honour what they saw of Him in His servant: when the church needed repairing, it was these young men from the bush who cut all the coral needed to build a new platform and staircase.

So instead of chafing because he was not pioneering, Tamate worked steadily on for another five years in Raratonga. His turn was to come, but certainly the steady work of that time taught a reckless man the meaning of prudence, and gave a man who was very forthright and outspoken the tactfulness which is needed to lure men to Christ: and probably the understanding he gained of how these islanders' minds worked, saved his life time and time again in the years to come.

During those ten years, how Tamate and Jeanie came to love and honour the native teachers! They weren't intellectual men, any of them: they knew only one book well, but it was the Book of books.

These Christian teachers—and their wives—were so thankful for their own deliverance from heathenism that they gladly endured exile from their homeland, sickness and danger of death from appalling climates, in some cases martyrdom at the hands of the cannibals. No difficulty or peril was great enough to hinder their longing to take to the other islands the Good News which had come to Raratonga.

How could a man like Tamate, a woman like Jeanie, not long to share the privilege which several of the men and women they had trained were already enjoying? But their waiting time came to an end, at last: in 1877, when Tamate was still only thirty-six, the word was given to go, and he and Jeanie set out for Papua, in New Guinea.

VI

REAL CANNIBALS

"IF anyone visiting the shores of New Guinea is clubbed to death, his friends may have the satisfaction of knowing that the deed was done with the best ebony!" That was the sort of thing people said about Tamate's "promised land."

There were the wildest rumours abroad about the richness and wealth of the country: but everyone knew as sober fact what the people were. They were degraded, cruel, murderous. Although only a few hundred miles of water separated the island from Australia, the Australians—who were never lacking in courage—left it severely alone.

This was the place where Tamate was to do his finest work. At long last, after ten patient years of useful service—useful to the mission, useful to Tamate and Jeanie—the great adventure had really begun.

The mission supplies were put on board the mission ship *Bertha*, and they set off with a Mr. Macfarlane, another missionary, from Murray Island.

Their first sight of New Guinea was uninviting: they anchored near a place called Boera, where Piri, a native teacher, had been established for some time. But if the place was unattractive, at least they were welcomed. They found at Boera not only Piri, but Mr. Lawes, who was now stationed at Port Moresby, the chief mission on New Guinea, with his wife.

Piri and his wife had built themselves a comfortable house, and they had already erected a small but delightful little church, which also had to serve as a school.

Living with Piri and his wife were the widows of two other native teachers who had given their lives in the Master's work—not in any dramatic way, but simply by enduring to the last the terrible climate.

These two women were taken on to the mission ship that they might settle down with Tamate and Jeanie: then the *Bertha* set sail for Port Moresby, followed by Piri and his wife in a large canoe.

Port Moresby was unattractive, too: it was a burnt-up, barren looking place, swampy and uninviting. But Tamate and Jeanie stayed there with Mr. and Mrs. Lawes for a few days. Tamate and Mr. Macfarlane took a trip inland to explore the mountain country. They made quite a large party: they took with them Ruatoka, the native teacher at Port Moresby; some natives from the station; four other teachers who were on their way eastward: and there was a Mr. Goldie, a naturalist, as well.

The first day they did not meet a soul. They made for Mr. Goldie's camp, which was their first stop: it was close to a large river, and Tamate would have dearly loved a swim. But there were none of them willing to keep company with numerous alligators, and so the natives poured water over the white men instead—a far safer method, if not quite so refreshing!

After that they slung their hammocks in the bush and rested for a while, then pushed on again until sunset. Again their hammocks were slung in the trees: and a strange night they passed. The natural inhabitants of the region—wallabies which leaped past, the unknown birds overhead— all mistrusted the intruders in their peculiar-looking nests; and when the exploring party began to sing their evening hymns there was consternation among the furred and feathered company.

They were up before dawn, and soon they began to meet formidable looking armed natives: but when Ruatoka shouted, *"Misi Lao, Misi Lao!"* (the native name for Mr. Lawes) they put down their spears and came running to meet them.

These were strange people. They not only chose to live on the tops of the mountain ridges, but they also built their homes in the tops of the highest trees: and very unsafe they looked, with crude plank platforms spread unsteadily across the branches for their only "foundations."

The people were soon good friends with the intruders, some smoking tobacco, some chewing bright red betel-nuts, which stained their mouths and teeth to a most exotic shade.

There was a sensation when Tamate, by now tanned to a deep, rich brown, changed his shirt. When they saw his white skin—and the kind of skin which freckles is generally *very* white—they raised a great shout, and crowded round to see the strange sight.

Tamate and one or two others decided to explore a little farther before going back to Port Moresby, but now they could no longer use Mr. Lawes's name as a passport. Still, Tamate was not daunted, not even when they unexpectedly met a party of truly terrifying natives. Their dark faces were blackened with a revolting paste of soot and gum, and were then sprinkled over with a white powder. Their mouths and teeth were vividly red from betel-nuts, their eyes flashing with alarm and suspicious anger; and their spears were poised to deal death to the strangers.

But Tamate and the others made a variety of strange signs to express their harmlessness, and finally the savages were reassured, and became quite friendly.

The journey back down the mountainside in the early dawn was another strange experience. Fireflies danced in their thousands ; many birds, disturbed before their usual waking-time, gave out squawks and screeches and then settled down to sleep again.

It was midday before they reached Port Moresby again, tired and footsore, Tamate at least grumbling at the footwear shoemakers supplied to exploring missionaries.

"Wish they had the wearing of them themselves," he grumbled to Jeanie, as he pulled his boots gingerly off his sore, aching feet.

After a few days' rest Mr. Macfarlane set off again in the *Bertha*, taking Jeanie with him, to visit the native teachers on the coast: Mr. Lawes and Tamate followed in a small seven-ton schooner the *Mayri*. This time they were voyaging in search of a suitable place for Tamate's headquarters.

On the way they visited several of the native teachers along the coast, and then they began to put in at new, untouched places where no white man had ever been before.

They found the people very, very suspicious: they had only to enter a village for the men to arm at once, and the women to disappear into the bush. But they grew more trustful, when the missionaries had shown their good intentions in the approved New Guinea fashion—by taking hold of their own noses and pointing to their stomachs!

Soon the *Bertha*, with Jeanie still on board, joined up with the *Mayri* again, and together they sailed eastward. They noticed that the farther they went away from Port Moresby the finer the country became: the people, too, were better built and lighter-skinned, and some of the boys and girls were really delightful little people to look at.

It was not easy to find just the right spot for the mission: some places were obviously unhealthy, some had a poor water supply, some were unsafe for those more human reasons which carry particular weight where the inhabitants of a land are all cannibals.

But at last they came across the ideal place. They had not expected to find it where they did. Tamate had gone in the boat with the captain of the *Bertha* just to find an anchorage.

But they found a splendid bay, and on the bay was a man fishing. They soon pulled toward him, to his very great terror: but when Tamate held up a piece of red cloth and some beads, indicating by the usual attentions to his nose and his stomach that his intentions were good, the native was at last reassured. But he was an evil-looking man: for an ornament he wore on his arm a human jaw-bone! Tamate was to see that man again later.

But at least he was no longer afraid: he paddled off home, and the ship's captain with Tamate rowed back to the *Bertha* and showed her the way in to good anchorage.

It was still early afternoon, and soon the ship was surrounded by a number of canoes. It was not a peaceful sight, this bevy of canoes filled with shouting, gesticulating men, all armed with spears. But they were not actively hostile, and at last some of them were persuaded to venture on deck.

No one could distrust what they saw there. Calm and quiet Jeanie sat there *knitting!* Soon one old man grew very friendly with her: "Kirikeu! Kirikeu!" he introduced himself.

"Tamate Vaine! Tamate Vaine!" Jeanie responded softly; that meant Mrs. Tamate: and soon they were carrying on a sign conversation. Before the evening was over Kirikeu made it quite plain that he was going back home to have a sleep, but in the morning he would return with a gift of food for the white lady.

The missionaries would not allow any of the canoes to stay by the ship after dusk, and they kept a careful watch all night: one canoe did approach long before daylight, but the man was warned off and they were left in peace until dawn.

Kirikeu was in the very first canoe to come alongside at sunrise, and he had remembered his promise, and brought some taro with him. Naturally enough he was given a present in return.

Soon many more natives came on board, some of them not disinclined to quarrel, several of them adorned with human bones by way of jewellery. But somehow the peace was kept, and after breakfast the missionaries, under Kirikeu's leadership, went ashore to look for a suitable spot for the mission station.

For Tamate had made up his mind that this lovely bay was ideal for his purpose. It was a healthy site—as far as any site on New Guinea could be healthy—and was surrounded by villages whose inhabitants were certainly in sore need of the Gospel. The fact that they were cannibals, whose friendliness was questionable, and whose trustworthiness was non-existent, was quite beside the point.

Kirikeu found them just the right position. Between two small villages was a piece of land with a point of white sand running down to black rocks at the water's edge.

There was fresh water in the bush behind, and a little way along the beach a spring, which, Kirikeu told them, never dried up.

They held a consultation with the local chief, who agreed that the missionaries might build there. They asked him, too, for the use of a house while they built, but unfortunately he would only let them have one end of his own residence.

It was very kind of him, and they could not refuse his hospitality. But they were separated from his family by a partition about two feet high. The floor was littered with the bones of pigs and birds and fish, and hanging on the walls—just to remind them of their whereabouts—were human skulls, and a liberal supply of clubs, spears and shields.

The first night it was uncanny to see the moonlight on these treasures: and it was unmistakably unpleasant when at three o'clock in the morning the chief stepped over the partition to inspect his guests and their belongings.

Perhaps the native teachers were the most comfortable members of the party, for they slept on the shore in makeshift tents rigged up from some old sailcloth.

Needless to say they soon got to work on the

mission house. That very morning Tamate rowed out to the *Bertha* and came back with a supply of tomahawks and knives—the currency in which wages would be paid.

It was easy to make the villagers of Suau— that was the name of the district—understand what kind of wood was wanted; soon the knives and axes were given out, and a wildly excited but pleased company sallied forth into the bush to chop and hack with the white man's weapons.

Before long there was a good supply of timber on the beach; the space for the house was measured out, twelve yards by six, and holes were dug for the posts.

While this was being done Tamate rowed to and from the *Bertha*, bringing the teachers' own possessions to shore.

The first Sunday the missionaries spent at Suau must have seemed a strange day to the natives. The missionaries held their service under a great tree near the chief's house, the very tree where their cannibal feasts had been held.

Of course the people did not hide the fact that they were cannibals. Human flesh was very good to eat, they said. One man Tamate talked with was very emphatic on this point.

"Is man *good* to eat?" Tamate asked him.

"You savee pig?" was the return question.

"Yes."

"Well, no good. You savee sheep?"

"Yes," Tamate answered again.

"Well, no good. Man he too much good!" and he smacked his lips.

It was among people like that that Tamate was beginning to build his home—the first home, as a matter of fact, that he and Jeanie had had for their very own.

But they were in good health, and longing to get to work. When their house was nearly ready they watched the *Bertha* sail away without a qualm. The *Mayri* was anchored in sight still, but except for the teachers and their wives they were quite alone among the savages.

They were unafraid, but they were reasonably cautious. The natives were a very "having" people: axes, knives, hoop iron, beads, cloth and tobacco—these were wonderful treasures to them: so Tamate kept his stores of barter safely out of sight on the *Mayri*, and only landed such things as he needed.

As it was, serious trouble was only prevented at the outset because Tamate was as brave as a lion, firm and unflinching.

He had been working on the house, and found that he needed a saw which was on board. So he went down to the water's edge and shouted to the native captain of the *Mayri*:

"Look in my tool box, and find my saw, and send it ashore, will you?"

At that moment he heard a sound behind him, and turning he faced an armed, ugly looking mob of painted savages.

With a hasty gesture to the captain to stay

where he was, Tamate made a sudden rush which carried him through the crowd, and dashed to the front of the chief's house.

Angry men can be very eloquent without speaking an intelligible word. By means of furious signs the mob made it quite plain that only generous gifts of axes, knives and hoop iron would induce them to refrain from murdering the whole missionary party.

Well to the fore was a particularly ill-looking specimen, wearing a human jaw-bone, and carrying a heavy stone club. *It was the man who had been fishing in the bay when Tamate first landed.*

Tamate looked him straight in the eye, and not caring whether he understood the words or not, he demanded in loud, angry tones:

"What do you want?"

Enraged gestures answered him: presents or death, death for them all.

"You may kill us, but never a thing will you get from us!" Tamate returned firmly: again the man understood his meaning, and his looks grew even more threatening.

The teachers were timid: "Give them just something!" they implored.

Even Kirikeu gave the same advice. "They come from the other side of the island," he said. "Give them something and they will go away!" His meaning, too was clear enough, although he didn't express it in English.

But Tamate knew well enough what would happen if he gave in at that point. Somehow he had an inner conviction that this was not to be the end of all his long years of training for taking the Gospel to New Guinea. "I was in quite a don't care mood!" he wrote when telling the story after it was all over.

"Let them do it now, and be done with it!" he exclaimed hardily, but without taking his eye off the crowd. "Once we begin there will be no end to it. And my friend," he turned to Kirikeu, "I never give presents to people carrying arms. We have never carried arms among them, and we live here as their friends!"

Kirikeu did them good service, talking to the crowd fast and furiously; and the chief supported him. At last with many angry mutterings they retired to the bush behind the house to talk the matter over.

After much discussion they sent their representatives, still armed, to the chief's house, speaking more politely it is true, but still demanding presents.

Tamate was adamant. "I never give to armed people," he repeated, and went indoors without another sign, to continue in prayer with Jeanie and the teachers.

The deputation disappeared into the bush again, and the rest of the uneasy afternoon passed. Naturally no more work was done that day, and through the night a watch was kept.

There was a good deal of unrest, with the natives moving about in the bush, but nothing else happened.

"Work again this morning," Tamate announced briskly after breakfast: and he boldly led his heavy-eyed fellow-workers out to the half-finished tasks. They were soon at work putting on the wall plates of plaited coconut leaves, working vigorously enough in spite of the sleeplessness and fears of the night.

They had not long been busy before Kirikeu appeared, accompanied by a clean, unarmed, and rather sheepish native.

"This is the chief of yesterday," Kirikeu introduced him, "and he is sorry for what took place!"

So peace was made for the time. Tamate talked with him—still, of course, by signs—and took him to the chief's house to find him a present—a small one so that there should be no misunderstanding—but still a present, as he was now friendly, and carried no weapon.

Through it all Jeanie was brave and trustful. She soon gained the affection of the people. The workmen grew to like the sight of her, sitting on the platform in front of the chief's house sewing or knitting; every day a young warrior, wearing the shell ornaments which marked him out as a fighting man, would come and sit in front of her.

They had an arrangement which suited them both. The fierce young warrior taught the Scottish lady his language, and she taught him to knit!

VII

"IF WE DIE, WE DIE"

At last the day came when the mission house was finished, and it was time to move from the chief's house. This was a time of more anxiety, for Tamate well knew that when the natives set eyes on his and Jeanie's possessions, they would be covetous eyes.

When the moving day came the natives stood round eyeing the proceedings. Twice spears and clubs were raised.

"The things in our chief's house belong to us!" they affirmed angrily.

But Tamate was firm, and the mission property was at last moved into the mission house. Many things were stolen, but he thought it was wise to turn a blind eye to petty thieving. The plain truth was that there was so much of it among these people that had they made a crisis of every theft, life would have been one long series of upheavals.

So a present was given to the chief as an expression of thanks for his hospitality, and of course he was paid for the use of his house and the ground where the teachers' tent had been erected.

By now the natives were beginning to depend upon the fact that the missionaries were their friends. Many of them brought vegetables and fish, and were suitably rewarded. They honoured Tamate by invitations to share their feasts— cannibal feasts—and one day Kirikeu presented Jeanie with a special tit-bit: it was breast-of-man, already cooked!

One of the chiefs even offered Tamate his elder daughter as a sort of spare wife: Tamate must have more than one wife if he were to be a great chief! Tamate's wife was, of course, very fine, very good, but she was only one . . .

But Tamate seemed quite content with his one lady, and instead of extending his household he began to extend his property. He bought a piece of land for planting purposes, and in spite of the fact that by now he and Jeanie were suffering from fever, he was soon clearing the bush.

They could now understand much of what was said to them by the Suau people, and make themselves understood: and Tamate was beginning to make short trips of exploration.

Not long after the house was finished he made up his mind to go to a place called Tepauri. The people there were bitter enemies of the Suau tribes, and Tamate hoped to make peace.

"You not go, Tamate! You not go!" the people implored him, especially Kirikeu. "We have fought with them, killed them, and eaten their bodies. They have not been paid for, and as you are our great friend, your head would be considered good payment. Will you go now?"

"Yes, I go tomorrow morning. God will take

care of us," and he went, taking with him Beni, the only teacher who was a widower. It did not seem to occur to Tamate that he himself was not a widower.

They went in the *Mayri*, and when they came to Tepauri Tamate and Beni, with one native from the schooner, rowed to land. Ashore was a noisy crowd of armed natives; so that the boat should not be stolen Tamate told the man to row her back to the *Mayri* while he and Beni waded ashore.

The minute they reached dry land a crowd of natives were dancing round them, shouting unintelligibly; clubs and spears were very much in evidence.

They were seized by the hand and hurried along the beach. Tamate protested and resisted, but it was no good: there was no escaping the firm grip of those dark brown hands. Beni was in the same plight, and they were hustled along, the crowd keeping up a swinging dance round them, waving clubs and spears, and pretending to throw them, or to strike blows.

One word only could they make out, "*Goira! goira!*" Now in Raratongan the word "*koia*" means, "Spear them!" so the missionary and the teacher feared the worst.

Soon they came to a dry watercourse, leading, of course, inland. Up this they dragged their unwilling captives.

But here the going was rougher: Tamate thrust a foot against the first good-sized rock he came to, and Beni was quick to imitate him. That arrested their progress for a moment, but only for a moment: they were both subjected to the indignity of being lifted over the obstacles!

"Beni," Tamate shouted over his shoulder. "You try to get back. They may let *you* go!"

"I've tried, but it's no use," Beni panted.

"Well, what d'ye think's happening?"

"Oh," Beni answered despairingly, puffing and panting the while, "they are taking us to their place of ceremony to kill us!"

"Looks like it," Tamate assented grimly. "Ah well, Beni, it's no use resisting. God is with us, so let us go quietly."

So they marched meekly on until they reached a hill, and there, near to a large rock was a little rivulet, dropping into a pool below. It was a tiny paradise, rich with moss and fern and lichen. Was it to be the ironical setting of yet another missionary martyrdom?

Tamate was set on one rock near the pool, Beni on another. Then there was silence. What strange sacrificial rite was this?

Then Tamate's captor spoke: a positive harangue it was, and it was not easy to understand. But careful listening, and their combined knowledge of Raratongan and the New Guinea languages soon made all plain.

When Tamate landed at Suau his first demand had been for good water—what the Tepauri people called "*goira.*" Well, here was water.

"Tamate, look! There is good water. It is yours, and all this land is yours, and our young men will

begin at once to build you a house. Go and fetch
your wife and leave that bad, murdering lot you
are now among at Suau, and come and live with
us!"

So ended a false alarm. The Tepauri people
entertained them, and saw them safely back on
board the *Mayri*: and though Tamate did go back
to the "bad murdering lot," they parted the best
of friends.

The Suau people would not come near the
mission house for a little while, but finally a few
plucked up courage: "They did not kill you then,
on Tepauri: *but did you eat anything?*"

"Oh, yes, plenty!" and Tamate rubbed his
person appreciatively.

The Suau people were shocked, horrified:
"They will have poisoned you!" they exclaimed:
there were many I-told-you-so looks the next
day when Tamate was taken ill. But it was only
a slight attack of fever, and they were reassured.
Tamate was delighted: the feud was over!

The next excitement was actually on Suau,
and it was much more serious. Tamate was bush-
clearing, and the teachers were down on the shore
sawing up some of the wood. One of the crew of
the *Mayri* was also ashore, getting wood and
water for the schooner, when Tamate noticed
that as he gathered wood he worked his way closer
and closer.

Soon he was within hearing: "I think we going
have trouble!" he muttered. "Natives all look
bad, and been off trying make row we fellow."

Tamate thought it was a false alarm, but New Guinea was not the place in which to take any risks. At once he called the men off from the work. It was as well: only a minute or two later he heard a commotion from the *Mayri*, where only the cook and the captain were now on board: the rest of the crew were down by the boat.

Somehow the natives on shore had rowed out in their canoe, boarded the *Mayri*, and got hold of the long cable which was kept on deck: others were in the water pulling up the anchor, and in a few minutes they would have her in to the shore, at their mercy.

The rest of the crew were shouting from the dinghy, because the natives would not let them launch her to go to the *Mayri's* rescue.

Tamate was down on the beach in a moment. Like a whirlwind, utterly fearless, he ran to the boat and sent the troublesome natives flying. In a trice he had leaped in and grabbed the oars, and she was afloat.

These fierce cannibals had acquired a very healthy respect for their missionary. It was not that he bullied or blustered, or used his hands, nor that he went armed; it was just the sheer power of the man: and when the men on the deck of the *Mayri* saw him coming toward them, a bronzed, bearded figure with a very angry, determined face, they let go of the anchor, and slipped overboard.

They could not face him; they joined their fellows on the shore, and from the deck of the

Mayri Tamate could see an angry crowd gathering round the mission house, all with spears and clubs.

There was trouble on board, too. In the struggle over the anchor one man had been killed—and sadly enough it was the young warrior who had been helping Jeanie with the language—and the captain had been wounded.

That death was a serious matter, a matter which might cost the lives of the whole missionary party. Tamate did what he could: already the natives still on board were making ready to take the body of the dead man ashore, but if they reached land before the missionary did, all hope would be gone.

Kirikeu's son was fortunately there, and he managed to persuade the angry natives to wait until Tamate was back on land, so that he had a chance to explain the whole affair to the people before the body was brought ashore. Had he not done so there would have been a massacre at once—and a cannibal feast that night: "Man he too much good!"

The chief Suau people assured Tamate that they would not let the missionary party be harmed, but they were not at all to be relied upon. There was a great wailing and many angry looks, much waving of spears and clubs, when the body was landed: out in the bay they could see more and more canoes from villages along the coast crowding in.

By dusk Tamate had made all his arrangements. He sent a message to the *Mayri* for them to send out all the barter that could be spared, and then to stand in readiness to leave at a moment's notice.

While he was giving his orders, a native crept through the bush to speak to him:

"Tamate!" he whispered urgently, "you must get away tonight if you can. At midnight, perhaps, you may have a chance. Tomorrow morning when the big star arises they will murder you!"

In the deepening dusk there was serious consultation in the mission house. Tamate reported on all the happenings of the day, explaining just what had occurred and what it might mean, and telling of this latest warning.

He turned to Jeanie: "It is for you to decide," he told her. "Shall we men stay and you women go—for there is not room for us all on the *Mayri?* Shall we try all of us to go *somehow?* Or shall we all stay?"

Jeanie was calm, as she had been all day, and outwardly at least as little afraid as her husband.

"We have come here to preach the Gospel and do these people good," was her answer, given in no uncertain tone. "God will take care of us. We will stay. If we die, we die. If we live, we live!"

With such an example of quiet heroism, what could the teachers' wives do but follow her example?

"Let us live together, or die together," they exclaimed.

"It's time for evening prayers, then," Tamate said in matter-of-fact tones, for he dared not show how deeply he was moved. "It won't be wise to sing . . ."

As Tamate was praying in Raratongan dialect there was a clanking sound from the bay: it was the *Mayri* pulling up anchor according to the orders he had given: and as he finished he could see the last of her going out of the bay. Now the missionaries, the teachers and their wives were quite alone in the little mission house, surrounded by hordes of angry savages, shielded by a fence so low that a man could leap over it, *and by the care of God.*

During the long, anxious night there was little disturbance; but with the morning light there came the ugly sound of many war-horns, calling in more and more natives from the surrounding villages.

At four o'clock the chief came to the mission house and conferred with Tamate, and he was shown the parcels of gifts which the missionary and Jeanie had made up in the night, to give as compensation to the friends of the dead man.

"It is not enough," the chief affirmed stonily.

"If you will wait till the big steamer comes," Tamate told him—glad of the chance to let the natives know that the *Mayri* would be returning, and accompanied by a steamer: "I may be able to give you more."

"We must have more *now*!" the chief demanded angrily.

"I cannot give you more now."

Tamate could say no more: there was nothing

else to say. The chief went away, and they made themselves ready for immediate attack.

But it did not come. Several times the natives came as far as the fence and shouted demands for more presents, but when they were ignored they went away again.

That day was Sunday, and a strange Sunday it was. All through the day and the next night the mission party had to keep a strict watch: on the Monday when the poor victim was buried and the grisly funeral feast held, they thought the attack *must* come.

Monday passed in the same tense atmosphere, and Monday night came. It was when Tamate had just finished his spell of watching and had fallen asleep at three o'clock, that Jeanie woke him, shouting:

"Quick! They have taken the house!"

He sprang from his bed and rushed to the door —which was nothing more substantial than a piece of native cloth. There in the dim morning light he saw one large armed party standing in front, and one at the side of the house.

It was a terrifying moment, but Tamate was still unfaltering.

"What do you want?" he demanded, as he had asked so often.

"Give us more compensation," their leader said menacingly, "or we will kill you and burn the house *now*!"

"Kill you may," Tamate replied, "but no more compensation do I give. Remember, if we die,

we shall die fighting: and there is an end
of it!"

He turned on his heel and beckoned to the chief
to follow him. Oddly enough, this angry, savage
man meekly went after him into the house!

Tamate reached up to the rack on the wall
where his musket rested: in silence he took it
down and charged it with powder and shot.

"You have seen us shoot birds with this," he
said at last, tapping the weapon significantly.
"Go, tell your friends that *we are going to fight*.
There must be an end of this. The first man that
crosses where that fence stood" and he made a
wide sweeping gesture toward the broken fence,
"is a dead man!—Go!"

The chief went. For over an hour the natives
had a discussion, and then once more the chief
came toward the house.

"Tamate!" he called.

"*Back!*" Tamate roared. "No one comes inside
that fence again!"

"Tamate, it's all right!" the old man said
urgently. "Look!" And there out on the bay
Tamate saw a large war canoe manned, and
several hundred smaller ones being lifted into
the water.

It seemed almost too good to be true, but it
happened. Soon the canoes were disappearing
from the bay, and there was quietness at Suau.

The Suau chief had decided that a live Tamate
with a helpful wife, and teachers, a schooner full
of treasures, was better than a dead Tamate and

a cannibal feast which would, after all, be all
forgotten in a day or two: especially in view of
the fact that an attack would be at the price of
at least one life, and that might be his own.

So by arguments and persuasions he had
induced the men from the surrounding villages
to go away: as for his own people, he could deal
with them, he hoped! and he did.

You see, there was too much work to be done
for God in New Guinea for James Chalmers to
come to the end of his life just yet: the Lord saw
to it that His servant *could* go on working.

VIII

JEANIE

LIFE in those days was never particularly safe
for white people among the cannibals of the South
Seas, but from that time onward Tamate and
Jeanie lived in the Suau district in what they
considered as safety: though for the first few weeks
after the disturbance they were warned not to
wander too far from home.

There was plenty to do near the mission house:
bush-clearing, fencing, planting, church and
school building, as well as the work which is so
often called *proper* missionary work: that of
preaching to the people, holding services, teaching
the grown-ups and the boys and girls to read and
write; translating the Bible.

It was probably in the more everyday work that they won the confidence of the people. They could see that their Tamate and his wife, the teachers and their wives, could work happily together and keep good-tempered. They could see their friendliness, and that they were willing to trust them. But when Tamate found he must go to Cooktown for fresh supplies, he was in a perplexity. At that time there was no suitable accommodation on the mission steamer for Jeanie, but how could he leave her?

Jeanie was in no doubt whatever. It was during the unhealthy season: the disturbance had happened only a short while since, so how could they leave the teachers there alone? Suppose they fell ill, who would care for them: suppose there was fresh trouble, who was to settle it? and that soft-voiced, timid-seeming woman calmly announced that she would not dream of anything but staying behind!

The fact that she would be the only white woman among a horde of practically naked savage cannibals, was just beside the point: it did not matter that only a few weeks before they had been besieged, with death very near to them.

"We came here for Christ's sake, and He will protect us," was the only comment she had to make.

He did protect them: but it was a time of lonely hardship for Jeanie. The people were delighted that she should stay, and before Tamate had gone a day they were saying to one another, "*They trust us*: we must treat them kindly. They cannot mean us harm, or Tamate would not have left his wife behind!"

Yet imagine how she felt! She knew that no danger would hinder her James from doing his duty; in fact danger had its own charm for him: and if he were killed, what would become of her?

If she were left alone, with a house full of possessions which all her fierce neighbours eagerly coveted, anything might happen. Even her body, and those of the Raratongan teachers and their wives, would be regarded as delicacies for a cannibal feast!

Jeanie was heroic: but she *knew* that God would look after her. There was only the low fence around the mission station, but years later one of the chiefs told Tamate that during the first, troubled days, when they had planned to murder the whole party, again and again some strange power held them back: they had only to step over that fence, but *they could not do it*.

Added to Jeanie's loneliness, there soon came sickness. Two of the teachers were down with fever, and although she was ill herself, she dragged herself from her bed to nurse and physic them.

The natives proved kind and thoughtful: they brought her presents of food, many of them; but they left them at the house and went away immediately, that she might not be troubled. When she could eat nothing they grew very concerned about her: Tamate must not think they had not cared for her. She must eat plenty, so that when he returned she might be looking well and strong.

At last he came back, and there were two or three peaceful weeks before he was off again. While he was away the second time, on a short trip, she showed more of her mettle.

One day from the mission house she suddenly heard a great commotion from the village, shouting and shrieking, and loud, angry voices.

"A fight! A fight!" the nearby people exclaimed, and hurried off that they might not miss the excitement.

Jeanie was soon after them: she ran out of the mission house, down the hill, and along the village street. The sight of furious men with upraised spears did not daunt her. She ran right into the middle of them, a woman, small and slight as she was, and stretching out a daring hand she laid hold of one of the upraised spears.

"*Put it down!*" she commanded: and he obeyed: "And you, too; and you; and you!"

One by one the spears were lowered, and the great dark savages stood sheepish before the little missionary woman. She turned to the rest of the crowd, and begged them to put an end to the fight, imploring them to keep the peace.

Because their savage hearts were brave, these men admired courage, and hardly a warrior among them refused to honour Tamate's indomitable little wife, who was not afraid, not even of their clubs and spears! The outcome was that they sat meekly on the ground, there and then, and made peace with fitting ceremony.

After Tamate came back this time he and Jeanie spent several happy and eventful weeks in the mission steamer, visiting more than a hundred villages along the coast: and in ninety of these villages the people had never seen a white man before.

The journey did Jeanie good, for her health had suffered from the Suau climate and the Suau happenings. The sea breezes were refreshing, and although Tamate had some narrow escapes ashore, he always came safely back to her, even after visiting the most unfriendly places.

There were other voyages later, where Jeanie could not come. For as the months went by she grew steadily weaker, and in October, 1878 Tamate was compelled to send her to Sydney for proper nursing and medical attention.

He went with her as far as Cooktown, but there they had to part. With a heavy heart he turned back to New Guinea, and one of the first entries in the journal he kept for her amusement, was his birthday greeting to "my ain lassie."

He had a delightful story to tell her. He sat there in the lonely little house on the Sunday evening, chuckling as he wrote of the service that morning.

One of the first arrivals at the church had been a native dressed in a shirt—and to these naked savages that was finery indeed. Soon the place filled up, and they were almost ready to begin worship when an indignant late-comer, a large man with a jacket in his hand, but nothing on, came striding in.

An angry survey of the congregation enabled him to find the wearer of his shirt. He marched over to him and ordered him to disrobe: there and then the boy had to stand up and submit to being undressed by only too willing helpers.

The stolen shirt was restored to its rightful owner, who calmly dressed himself, and then, sitting down, composed himself for worship.

But they were long, lonely days for Tamate. It was not so bad when he was out in the little boat exploring the coastline, making acquaintance with strange peoples, some of them friendly, some of them hungry for the white man's meat!

Tamate too had his turns of sickness in loneliness, and a sick man is not so good at looking after himself as a sick woman.

"I have had another dreadful attack of fever," he wrote. "I am now better, but my head is light. Eh, my ain Jeanie, I do miss you . . ."

But he had to get used to being without her, for God wanted her in heaven. In the February of the next year, when he was thirty-eight, she died: peacefully and contentedly she left this life behind; her only trouble was that she must leave Tamate too.

Poor Tamate: he was on his way to her when he learned the news—from a friend's newspaper! He saw only her grave in Sydney. The London Missionary Society wanted him to go home, but he asked only one thing: that he might be allowed to go back to his work.

Jeanie in her last letter had written, "On no account leave the teachers!" How could he fail her? Only the previous November twenty fresh workers had arrived from Raratonga and other islands, to witness in New Guinea, and they *must* have the support of the white missionary.

The Society naturally consented. What else could they do with a man who in the deepest sorrow could say, "People are remarkably kind and sympathising; still I want to be with my savage friends. May I live more for Christ, all for Christ, and Christ all"?

When a man is as affectionate as he is brave, as tender-hearted as he is resolute, there is no better cure for sore heartache than work, work, work.

IX

TAMATE VAINE

IT was seven years before Tamate left his work in New Guinea to go back to Great Britain, as the directors of the London Missionary Society wished.

They were seven years of valuable work: he had no heart for the Mission house at Suau, without Jeanie, and the teachers were well established there. So as he was voyaging and exploring most of the time, it was more convenient for him to live at Port Moresby with Mr. and Mrs. Lawes.

More and more of the wild people of New Guinea came to love and respect Tamate. He went everywhere. He did not keep only to the coastal regions now: he made long journeys inland. On one tramp alone he covered over five hundred miles, and climbed more than forty thousand feet. He saw sights, people and customs never before seen by white men. He climbed long, rickety ladders to visit people in their treetop houses. He laughed to see grown-up men scolding the rain, and even spitting at it to make it go away.

He slept in native houses, and was kept awake for hours by one man who, instead of counting sheep, told himself endless incidents of ancient family history to put himself to sleep: he went on, and on, in a low, monotonous chant, nearly driving Tamate desperate, and certainly not soothing himself into slumbers.

He went where the natives assured him his death was certain, and he came away again with the savages as his friends. He told these warriors that he wanted to see peace all along the coast of New Guinea: although fighting and murdering were among their chief joys, and their chief sources of honour, they meekly agreed to do his bidding—and many of them kept their word and fought no more.

While Tamate was opening up new ground,

paving the way for the establishment of new stations, Mr. and Mrs. Lawes were continually busy in Port Moresby. There they had opened an Institution, much like the one on Raratonga, for the training of Christians from New Guinea, that they might be sent out as teachers to their own people: they were all looking forward to the time when they could do without South Sea Island teachers, and send men of New Guinea to win the people of New Guinea for Christ.

Before the seven years were up Tamate's work was attracting official attention: he became a celebrity. The important people in the world of geography, the Australasian Geographical Society, were so much impressed when his journal was published—as his friends insisted that it must be— that they asked him to take charge of an expedition to explore New Guinea at their expense. But Tamate was a missionary, not a fame-seeker.

Then when the representative of the British Government made an official inspection of New Guinea, at the time the island was declared a colony of Great Britain, it was Tamate who went with him on his tour of the Protectorate.

So that by the time he was ready to return to Great Britain, he was quite a famous man in spite of himself, and he left behind him in New Guinea a chain of mission posts, each with its native or South Sea Island teacher, points of light all along the coast of a dark island.

They lionised him when he got home to Britain, and he didn't much like it. He had gone out a rather pale, freckled, clean-shaven youth of twenty-five or so: he came back a solid, thick-set bronzed man of forty-four, with an impressive beard, and thick curly hair: his voice was splendid, deep and rich, and with his flashing eyes and the thrilling story he had to tell, it was no wonder that the people flocked to hear him.

Flock they did. There were meetings everywhere, in churches, chapels, mission halls, schools, private houses, up and down the land: congregations, women's meetings, men's meetings, children, celebrities and nonentities, all wanted to hear Tamate's story.

But his heart found most comfort in an old friendship renewed. There lived in Retford a certain lady who had been one of Jeanie's closest friends. Lizzie Large she had been, and for long years after they had left England and she had married, she had written to them.

Then when Jeanie died, her letters stopped, until Tamate's journal was published. Then she had written to him again, and ever since they had kept up a happy, comfortable correspondence.

Naturally one of his first visits had been to Lizzie and her husband: and when her husband died Tamate was there at hand to comfort her.

By the time he was ready to leave England again for New Guinea, Tamate had seen a great deal of Lizzie: and he did not set sail without good reason to hope that as soon as he was settled down again she would come out to him to be his wife.

Fifteen months passed before he was ready for her. Meantime he had a wonderful welcome when he got back to New Guinea: there was shouting and laughter and tremendous excitement long before the vessel reached the shore, and when Tamate landed . . . Well the dear old lady who threw her arms around his neck, and rubbed her black face all over his bronzed one, in a rapture of delight, was only doing what every man, woman and child would have liked to do.

Mr. and Mrs. Lawes were less demonstrative, but they were every bit as delighted to see him. There were a thousand and one questions to be asked: about their friends and the churches in the homeland, about Lizzie, and of course Mrs. Lawes must know exactly what she was like; equally of course Tamate was quite unable to tell her. What sort of meetings had he had? What sort of a voyage?

Tamate, too, must ask his questions. How was the work going on, in New Guinea and the other islands? How were the teachers, especially the new teachers . . ?

There was a silence, rather a sad silence. Then Mr. Lawes told a sad story. Of course in some places the work was progressing steadily, but one of Tamate's most dearly loved teachers, Tauraki, whom he had stationed at Motumotu, had been murdered with his wife and child. The teacher who helped him there had died of fever . . .

Being Tamate, he chose the scene of the recent

murder for his first visit: he was going to make peace, he announced, and off he went.

He needed the loving, excited welcome he received at the mission at Motumotu, to comfort him for his disappointed hopes. When he left the place nearly eighteen months ago he had had great hopes of what he would find when he came back: two splendid teachers, and a friendly people . . . Now he must begin all over again.

But soon he was making plans, plans which he shared with Lizzie when he wrote to her. There was enough wood ready sawn to make a large house for her future home, he said, and although there was fever everywhere, it was not worse than in other places! It was a good thing that Lizzie, like Jeanie, was built to the heroic model.

Then for a time the wanderer had to go back to Port Moresby to settle down to life on the station, not going very far afield. For Mr. and Mrs. Lawes were due for leave, and once they sailed Tamate must superintend the station work, not only teaching in the Institution and the school, seeing to the repair and strengthening of houses and gates, the care of boats, but even acting as commander-in-chief to the women in their sweeping, washing, weeding, and other work.

He was lonely; soon he was ill, and when he was ill he just could not touch the food the natives cooked: at last he grew hungry again, and staggered from his bed to a bookshelf to see if Mrs. Beeton's Cookery Book could help him! But Mrs. Beeton is far too advanced for a mere helpless male, so poor Tamate laid her aside in despair and went hungry.

But he was soon up and about again, and within a few days he was writing to Lizzie deploring the fact that *he was not a good needlewoman:* he did *so* want to teach the girls on the station to sew!

The time passed, and at last in October 1888 news came that Lizzie would soon be at Cooktown. Other missionaries had come to take over at Port Moresby, and so Tamate set sail in the mission steamer *Harrier*, to meet his bride.

Lizzie's ship had hardly anchored before she was swept on to the *Harrier* by a delighted, impetuous Tamate. Then he disappeared to make arrangements with a parson, and came back to tell her she must be ready for the wedding within an hour.

"It was capital fun to see the state she got in," wrote the naughty Tamate: "The bride was rushed!"

It was a good thing the voyage from England had been comfortable, and that Lizzie was in good health. For the voyage on the *Harrier* to New Guinea was simple misery to her. The vessel was given to rolling, and the poor bride only left her berth once, when the captain kindly anchored under the lee of an island so that the seasick lady might have at least one night of rest.

But once they came in sight of New Guinea all was forgotten: her first sight of the island included a glorious view of the mountains—which were not always to be seen from the sea—and she could think of nothing but the loveliness of the prospect, and of the lagoon, as she was rowed across it.

When they reached land troops of people came to meet them: the teachers and their wives, neatly dressed; a crowd of village people, the men with a piece of string round the waist, the women in grass petticoats, and the children in nothing at all.

It was just two months after their wedding that they left Port Moresby for Motumotu. They went by whale boat, and after a long, tedious voyage they arrived at three o'clock in the morning.

Poor Lizzie! Twenty-six hours that voyage had lasted, and during that time she had only had a few biscuits and some coconut milk to drink. No wonder she was too ill to walk when they did arrive: no wonder she was reluctant to get out of the boat on to the river bank where there were alligators in plenty!

It was pitch dark, and the shouting of the boats' crews sounded uncanny. But it produced results. Soon came a crowd of wildly excited people, waving blazing torches, crowding round Tamate and Tamate Vaine (Mrs. Tamate) giving them welcome.

Four men came from the teachers' house with a rough sofa, covered with pillows. Tamate Vaine was helped on to this, and she relaxed with a sigh of relief, only to clutch frantically at the sides as she was lifted shoulder high and borne off into the darkness.

When she had entered her new home in this

novel fashion she looked around in the torchlight, quite dismayed. She wanted to go to bed: but there was no bed. She wanted to sit down, off that horrible sofa, but there was no furniture, only a few mats on the floor. She wanted food, but there was no kitchen. There were no doors, no windows, and in one corner their belongings were stacked up in cases securely nailed down: and Tamate Vaine was so tired.

But the teachers' wives did wonders in no time. Soon the missionaries' mattress was spread on the floor, the bed made up: mosquito nets were stretched across, and native mats were nailed up in the doorways.

Thankfully Tamate Vaine crept into bed, and then Tamate brought her a meal—a typical man's meal of cocoa, biscuits and marmalade. But Lizzie ate gratefully, and soon fell asleep to the sound of the roaring waves, which fifty yards away rolled up the beach with tremendous force.

In the morning she had a chance to inspect her new home more closely. The "splendid bungalow," the "delightful place," as Tamate had described it, was scarcely what she had imagined it to be. It was all so very, very crude.

The walls were made of roughly—very roughly —sawn planks which overlapped in such a manner as to form a series of innumerable tiny shelves all the way up to the roof. These little ledges provided splendid homes for a variety of insects: there were spiders, tarantulas, cockroaches, crickets, ants and mosquitoes. In the roof there were in the

daytime lizards in their armies, and at night bats:
the rats and mice, too, shared the missionary home,
and they were both lively and energetic!

"I believe you'd rather face a crowd of natives
than the insects in the house!" Tamate teased
her, not long after they had arrived, and it was
true. Tamate Vaine soon came to love the people.

The men were wild, powerful fellows, wonder-
fully ornamented as to hair and face and arms,
but wearing little else: many of them were really
handsome, and it puzzled her that the women
should be so unattractive. But all were pleased
with Tamate Vaine, and though she felt strange
the first day Tamate left her alone for a few
hours, she was unafraid.

Twenty of the big men gathered round the
verandah of the house, but they made no attempt
to come in. Soon Tamate Vaine mustered up her
courage and went out to them: she let them touch
her, shake hands with her, and they were delighted. Soon they were proudly showing her their
precious armlets and necklets, and one man
brought her a gift of fish, another some young
coconuts.

"I didn't feel afraid at all," she told Tamate
that evening. "I don't think I shall mind being
left with them when you go inland. But I shall be
terribly dull without you, Tamate. I can't even
talk with the teacher's wife yet!"

But she, and Tamate, soon began to pick up
the language of Motumotu, and in spite of fever
she never found the life uninteresting while he

was there. It was impossible to be dull with that man: he would gather the natives round him and take language lessons from them, and there would be shouts of laughter from them all at the ridiculous mistakes he made.

So they persevered with the work, preaching, teaching, language study, and for Tamate Vaine, the improvement of her home.

She had the house whitewashed and the posts painted blue: she hung pictures on the wall and spread her cheerful red tablecloth on the crude wooden table, and put gay cushions in their folding chairs.

Even Tamate, who had grown almost regardless of comfort, acknowledged that the home was now a pleasant place with "woman's notions all about," as he put it.

x

"HOPE TO LEAVE"

TAMATE and Tamate Vaine both felt they ought to stay at Motumotu, even although the climate was a very trying one. Tamate had extended his work fifty miles along the coast, stationing new teachers as he went. This work must be supervised, and he wanted to go still farther afield to open up the dangerous and even more unhealthy Fly River region—and Motumotu was the best centre for such operations.

Sometimes Tamate Vaine went with him on his tours inland: often she sailed with him on his shorter voyages: and sometimes she stayed behind alone.

Once she was alone for nine long weeks, with the whole burden of the work—by this time greatly increased—on her shoulders. She was very ill during that time, but struggled valiantly on so that Tamate was more than proud of her when he came back.

"She is a 'new chum' still," he wrote home proudly, "but she carried on every branch of the work quite in the 'old chum' style!"

The secret was that Tamate Vaine had come to love these wild people; indeed, she confessed that she always did get on better with rowdy folks than with tame, quiet ones.

Some of the wildest of the men at Motumotu would do anything that Tamate Vaine asked them, although they did not pretend to have any sympathy with the "mission of peace," as they called the Gospel.

But repeated attacks of fever had worn her out, and Tamate saw that she must have rest and change, so he took her with him on a tour of the South Sea Islands. First they went to Brisbane, and from there to Samoa, where they met the famous Robert Louis Stevenson: and "R.L.S." who had until then held a poor opinion of missionaries, could not speak too highly of James Chalmers.

They went to Raratonga, and it was a strange

mixture of pleasure and pain for Tamate Vaine to see the old home of her friend who was gone: but it was pure delight and pride to see the joy of the Raratongans at seeing their beloved Tamate again.

When they came back to Motumotu, cheered and refreshed, Tamate Vaine tasted something of the same welcome. The people were delighted to see them both, but she had left them in such poor health that they had feared she would never return, so their happiness was all the greater. They *did* love her, and they were very, very careful of her in Tamate's future absences.

Twice he was away for long spells, once when he was shipwrecked on his way to Cooktown; and again when he made a second visit of inspection to the Fly River region. For they had decided that the time had now come for them to make their base there, to open up the whole area, and settle more teachers.

On that second absence Tamate Vaine was very ill; she had to be lifted out on to the native couch while her bed was being made, and one day she felt someone behind her, gently stroking her hair and her forehead. She could not turn herself to see who was there, but she soon knew.

It was the great warrior chief, handsome, savage, Lahari, who had crept into the house: and as he saw that little weary white woman lying there so weak and ill, his big heart was filled with indignation—even indignation at his dearly loved Tamate.

Suddenly he broke out into abuse: "Tamate very bad, very bad husband indeed: no good to leave his sick wife so long when she have big sickness, and no one cook her Beritani food . . ."

The first person Tamate saw when he came back—two weeks early because he somehow had the feeling he was needed—was Lahari.

"He seized hold of me and told me everything he thought about me!" Tamate told his wife afterwards, a little ruefully.

Other attacks of fever followed, until it was plain that Tamate Vaine would certainly not be fit to go to the Fly River region until she had had a long, long rest. So it was decided that she should go back home to England while Tamate established the work, with Saguane as his base.

It was very hard to part. Life on New Guinea was so uncertain. But when a man and his wife are determined to put the Lord's work first, He gives them the courage to go, to stay, or to separate.

So Lizzie sailed for England, and Tamate sailed for the Fly River region. Saguane was deserted when he first landed there: the whole population had gone up the river for a heathen ceremony. So he at least had the opportunity of selecting his mission site without doubtful assistance.

The villagers returned next morning, but happily they were kindly disposed. The chief turned out of his house so that the white man might live there while his own home was being built; and within a few days the work was begun.

But it was three years before Tamate Vaine joined him. During that time he himself went to Britain for leave, and then returned to supervise the whole of the work of the western coast, before taking up his task at Saguane again.

It was a far, far harder field than Motumotu. At first Tamate Vaine was dismayed, when she did come out. The house was so rough, and the people! The men and women were mean, dirty, selfish, and the children were what she called "a handful," literally young savages, who if anything went wrong fought with tooth and nail.

But Tamate Vaine was a missionary, and this was how she looked at the situation: "Jesus loves them all, and oh, how they need His love. Tamate, bless him, seems to like them well, and shakes hands and puts his arm over their shoulders, and never minds dirt and disease."

So they worked on together through a long, heartbreaking year. Tamate fell and injured his leg, and he was ill with malaria and rheumatic fever. The people seemed quite indifferent to the message, and no sooner had the children learnt a little, than they would disappear for months, so that when they came back they had to begin learning all over again.

But it was not for nothing: at last Tamate was able to report: "Day is dawning with us!"

There were fourteen baptisms at that time, and the people began to give up their idols and their heathen charms. A year later, in 1900, more than a hundred were baptised on one day, and the people from the surrounding villages gathered together for a Communion service at which there were three hundred Christians.

The tide had turned. What had happened long years ago on Raratonga was beginning now in the Fly River region. But Tamate Vaine grew more and more weak, and it was only too clear that her task would soon be finished. Yet the Lord did not leave Tamate alone: just about this time there came a splendid recruit from England, Oliver Tomkins, who for the next few months was to Tamate what Timothy had been to Paul. So that when Tamate Vaine went to heaven, Tamate was not left alone and uncomforted.

Neither was it many months before they were all together again. For in April, 1901, what the world called a tragedy happened—if it ever is a tragedy when brave men die in their Master's service.

Tamate and Oliver Tomkins were all ready to visit a place on Goaribari Island called—of all fitting names—Risk Point. The day before he went Tamate wrote in one of his letters: "The sun is shining . . . and I feel cheered!" He might almost have known it was nearly time for him to go to "the place of laughter," which was the name one of his converts had given to heaven.

They set off in good spirits in the mission steamer *Niue*, with a Raratongan teacher, Hiro, a native chief, and ten mission boys, and im-mediately they anchored the ship was surrounded with canoes. That was nothing unusual, and when Tamate had persuaded them to go ashore till morning, promising to visit them in the morning, all aboard the steamer were well content.

But day had scarcely dawned before they were back again, in huge numbers, and their canoes were filled with an ominous collection of bows and arrows, clubs, bamboo knives and spears. Soon natives were swarming all over the *Niue*, crowding the decks so that there was no room to move.

It was not till Tamate announced his intention of going ashore—and Tomkins promptly announced that he was going too, and would not be dissuaded—that any of the natives would consent to leave the ship: and even then half of them stayed behind.

Hiro remained on board with the captain, but everyone else went in the whaleboat: the situation was delicate, but Tamate had pacified far too many antagonistic savages to be gravely concerned.

So he went ashore peacefully, and with Tomkins and a few of the natives he allowed himself to be led to Dopima, the village, leaving the rest of the boys with the whaleboat.

He knew nothing of the plot the Dopima chief had made with the people of ten surrounding villages, to massacre the whole mission party. So they went peacefully into the house where they had been invited to share a meal—of all foul, treacherous things: and if the scene which

followed was altogether unpeaceful, the missionaries knew nothing of it.

There was a massacre, ugly, savage murder.
But death was swift and merciful, and while the
savage scene was being enacted at Dopima, with
wild shouting and bloodthirsty exultation,
Tamate and Tomkins and the others were with
the Lord they had served.

The *Niue* was looted by the natives who had
stayed aboard, but they spared the lives of the
captain and the teacher, for some unknown
reason, certainly not a merciful one. So the *Niue*
steamed sadly back to civilisation, bearing the
heavy tidings.

Tamate was by now famous: Tomkins was a
young man at the beginning of his service. So
there was much talk of the "terrible tragedy,"
and to punish the offenders a Government
expedition went the round of the murdering
villages, destroying their "dubus" (the warriors'
'club houses') and burning their war canoes.

But it was realised by those who were on the
spot that Tamate's death, and the punishment
it drew forth, would probably mark the end of
these massacres, so that the work he had begun
would now go on unhindered.

So it wasn't really a tragedy: and for Tamate
it was a new beginning. He had not meant it
that way, but the last entry he made in the
Niue's log, almost the last thing he wrote, was
this: "Blowing and showers. *Hope to leave!*" He
left. He left for heaven.